THE DNA
OF A
GODLY HUSBAND

THE DNA
OF A
GODLY HUSBAND

Key Elements for Success...

DAVID SCOTT, ED.D., D.MIN.

PURPLE CHAIR BOOKS
AND EDUCATIONAL PRODUCTS, LLC.

PCB

Published by Purple Chair Books and Educational Products, LLC

First Printing, 2025

Copyright © David Scott, 2025

Scott, David 1969-

The DNA of a Godly Husband

By David Scott

ISBN: 978-1-953671-14-1

Self-Help/Inspirational

Printed in the United States of America

Interior designed by Md Al Amin (aminbookdesign@gmail.com)

Cover designed by Sadia A @sadia_coverz

To my beautiful and amazing wife and companion, the incomparable First Lady Tamara Scott, A.K.A. (The Boss)

Foreword

There are few titles more honored—and more misunderstood—than "husband." In a world of shifting definitions and diluted commitments, the biblical vision of husbandhood remains a sacred counterculture. It is not a role to perform, but a calling to embody. It is not about dominance, but about devotion. And it is not shaped by culture, but by Christ.

The DNA of a Godly Husband is more than a book—it's a blueprint for transformation. With pastoral wisdom, theological depth, and practical clarity, this work calls men back to the original design: to love as Christ loves (Ephesians 5:25), to lead with humility (Philippians 2:3–5), and to live with integrity (Proverbs 10:9). It does not offer shortcuts or surface-level advice. Instead, it invites men into the deep work of spiritual formation—where character is forged, legacy is built, and homes are healed.

What makes this book especially powerful is its voice. It is not written from a distance, but from the trenches—from the pulpit, the counseling room, the prayer closet, and the lived experience of a shepherd who has walked with men through both triumph and trial. It speaks with the authority of Scripture and the compassion of a pastor. It confronts without condemning, and it convicts without shaming.

Every chapter beats with the heart of Christ. Whether discussing emotional safety, servant leadership, sexual integrity, or spiritual warfare, the message remains clear: godly husbandhood isn't about perfection — it's about pursuit. Pursuing Christ, your wife, and a love that sacrifices daily.

If you are a husband, a pastor, a mentor, or a man preparing for marriage, this book will

challenge, equip, and transform you. It will call you to rise—not just as a provider or protector, but as a priest in your home. It will remind you that your marriage is not simply a relationship—it reflects the gospel.

So read slowly. Pray deeply. And allow the Spirit of God to rewire your heart with the DNA of a godly husband.

Rev. Dr. David Scott
Pastor, Teacher, Husband

Table of Contents

Introduction

Brothers in Christ,

Never forget that the privilege of being a mate and partner to your spouse is more than a role. On the contrary, it is a sacred calling.

Before you are a husband, you are a son—loved by the Father (1 John 3:1), redeemed by the Son (Ephesians 1:7), and empowered by the Spirit (Romans 8:11). And before marriage is a ministry, it is a mystery: "This is a profound mystery—but I am talking about Christ and the church" (Ephesians 5:32). The world may define husbandhood by cultural norms, romantic gestures, or financial provision. But Scripture calls us higher. It calls us to embody the love of Jesus in the most intimate and enduring relationship we will ever steward.

This book is not a manual—it's a mirror. It will not give you formulas, but it will provide formation because the DNA of a godly husband is not found in personality traits or marital techniques. It is found in the character of Christ, who "loved the church and gave himself up for her" (Ephesians 5:25). That character must be developed, not copied.

As a pastor, I've journeyed with men through the valleys of broken trust (Psalm 34:18), the deserts of emotional distance (Jeremiah 17:5–8), and the mountaintops of restored intimacy (Joel 2:25). I've seen marriages revived by grace, and I've wept over those that fell apart under neglect. But I remain convinced: when a man commits his heart to God, his home begins to heal. "Unless the Lord builds the house, the builders labor in vain" (Psalm 127:1).

This journey is not for the faint of heart. It will require humility (Micah 6:8), courage (Joshua 1:9), and a willingness to be transformed by the renewing of your mind (Romans 12:2). But if you're ready to become the kind of husband who prays with authority (James 5:16), listens with tenderness (James 1:19), leads with integrity (Proverbs 20:7), and loves with sacrifice (John 15:13)—then you're in the right place.

Let us start not with techniques, but with truth. Not with pressure, but with presence. And not with fear, but with faith. "Be on your guard; stand firm in the faith; be courageous; be strong. Do everything in love" (1 Corinthians 16:13–14).

Your marriage is your ministry. Your love is your legacy. And your transformation begins now.

Grace and peace,

Rev. Dr. D. Scott

CHAPTER 1:
DEVOTED TO CHRIST FIRST

A godly husband begins with a godly man. This chapter explores how personal devotion to Christ shapes every aspect of marriage. Through prayer, Scripture, and surrender, husbands learn to lead from the overflow of intimacy with God—because no man can love well unless he's loved deeply by the Father.

CHAPTER 1

Devoted to Christ First

The Foundation of Godly Husband-hood Is Personal Discipleship

Before a man can lead his wife in love, he must first be led by Christ in surrender. The strength of a godly marriage is not found in charm, charisma, or even compatibility—it is forged in the furnace of daily devotion. A husband's spiritual authority begins not in the pulpit or the paycheck, but in the prayer closet.

1. The Heart of Husband-hood: Christ Before Covenant

- **Marriage is not your first calling—discipleship is.**
  God did not create man to be a husband first, but a worshiper. The covenant of marriage is sacred, but it is secondary to the covenant of grace.

- **Your wife is not your source—Christ is.**
  When a man seeks emotional, spiritual, or identity fulfillment from his wife instead of his Savior, he burdens her with a weight she was never meant to carry.

- **Leadership flows from Lordship.**
  A man cannot lead his home well if he is not being led by Christ daily. Submission to Jesus is the soil from which sacrificial love grows.

2. Intimacy with God Fuels Intimacy with Your Wife

- **Spiritual intimacy precedes emotional intimacy.**
  When a man communes with God, he becomes more attuned

to the Spirit—and therefore more sensitive to his wife's heart, needs, and unspoken longings.

- **The fruit of the Spirit is the fragrance of a godly husband.**
  Love, joy, peace, patience, kindness, goodness, faithfulness, gentleness, and self-control (Galatians 5:22- 23) are not personality traits; they are spiritual evidence. They make a man safe, steady, and sacrificial. Every husband needs the gift, power, and fruit of the holy spirit.

- **Prayer cultivates presence.**
  A man who prays for his wife becomes more present with her. Intercession softens the heart, sharpens the mind, and strengthens the bond.

3. Daily Spiritual Disciplines That Shape the Heart

A man should practice disciplines. They are not legalistic checkboxes; they are lifelines. They shape the soul, renew the mind, and anchor the heart in Christ.

4. Building a Legacy of Devotion

- **Your children will learn husband-hood by watching your worship.**
  The most powerful sermon your family will ever hear is the one you live in front of them. This echoes the spirit of St. Francis of Assisi, who said, "Preach the Gospel at all times. When necessary, use words." Your life is the sermon. Kindness, integrity, gentleness, consideration, and generosity are the virtues learned without you saying a word.

- **Your wife will feel most secure when she sees you anchored in Christ.**
  Emotional stability, spiritual clarity, and moral integrity come from daily devotion. Most women want to feel safe and secure. Nothing guarantees safety and security like a man who follows God, seeks His guidance, and obeys His direction.

- **Your legacy begins with your altar.**
  Build one in your home. Make prayer normal. Make Scripture visible. Make Christ central.

Closing Exhortation:

Before attempting to repair your marriage, focus on deepening your relationship with Christ. Before trying to be understood, aim to understand God's heart. Before leading your wife, commit to following Jesus. A godly husband is not flawless, but he is engaged and fully committed. That commitment starts with Christ above all.

Reflection

CHAPTER 2:
NURTURER OF
COVENANT LOVE

Marriage is a covenant, not a contract. This chapter unpacks the biblical meaning of covenant love—faithful, sacrificial, and enduring. Husbands are called to reflect Christ's love for the Church, pursuing their wives with intentionality and protecting the sacred bond they share.

CHAPTER 2

Become a Nurturer of Covenant Love

Marriage is a Sacred Covenant, not a Consumer Contract.

Marriage is not a transaction; it is a transformation. It is not founded on convenience but on covenant. A godly husband does not simply cohabitate with his wife; he cultivates her heart, protects her dignity, and pursues her soul. To nurture covenant love is to mirror the relentless, sacrificial love of Christ.

1. Covenant vs. Consumer: A Kingdom Contrast

- **Consumer love says, "I'll stay as long as I'm satisfied."**
  Covenant love says, "I'm committed even when it costs me."

- **Consumer relationships are built on performance.**
  Covenant relationships are built on promise.

- **Marriage is not a contract to be negotiated—it is a covenant to be honored.**
  God designed marriage as a reflection of His unwavering love for His people (Malachi 2:14, Ephesians 5:31–32).

- **Covenant love is not reactive; it is proactive.**
  It initiates grace, forgives quickly, and chooses faithfulness daily.

2. Protect, Prioritize, Pursue: The Husband's Holy Charge

Protect Her!

- Guard her heart from emotional neglect, harsh words, and spiritual isolation.

10

- Be her safe place—emotionally, physically, and spiritually.

- Protect her reputation, her dreams, and her dignity in public and private.

Prioritize Her!

- Make her feel seen, heard, and valued above all earthly relationships.

- Schedule intentional time—date nights, prayer moments, shared dreams.

- Let her know she is not competing with your work, hobbies, or ministry.

Pursue Her!

- Don't stop courting her after the wedding.
  Pursuit is proof of value.

- Learn her love language—and speak it fluently.

- Ask questions that open her heart: "What's bringing you joy lately?" "How can I serve you better this week?"

3. Living Ephesians 5: Humility and Strength in Action

"Husbands, love your wives, just as Christ loved the church and gave himself up for her…" — *Ephesians 5:25*

- **Christlike love is sacrificial.**
  It lays down ego, agenda, and comfort for the sake of the beloved.

- **Christlike leadership is servant-hearted.**
  Headship is not domination; it is dedication. It means going first in forgiveness, first in prayer, first in humility.

- **Christlike strength is gentle.**
  It does not crush. It carries. It does not demand, it delights.

- **Christlike humility listens.**

  A godly husband listens not just to words, but to tone, silence,

  and emotion. He listens to God before he speaks to his wife.

4. Building a Home of Covenant Love

Practice	Description	Impact
Daily Blessing	Speak life over your wife each morning—affirm her identity, beauty, and worth	Builds emotional safety and spiritual intimacy
Weekly Check-In	Ask intentional questions about her heart, Stress, and dreams	Strengthens communication, and empathy
Monthly Vision Time	Pray together about your family's direction, goals, and spiritual growth	Aligns your marriage with God's purpose
Annual Renewal Ritual	Revisit your vows, write a letter, or take a retreat to renew your covenant	Rekindles passion and deepens commitment

Reflection

CHAPTER 3:
ANCHOR OF
EMOTIONAL SAFETY

E motional safety is the soil where intimacy grows. This chapter teaches husbands how to create a home where their wives feel secure, valued, and heard. Through empathy, active listening, and gentle strength, men become anchors in the emotional storms of life.

CHAPTER 3

Anchor of Emotional Safety

Creating a Home Where Your Wife Feels Seen, Heard, and Safe

Every woman longs for a sanctuary, a place where her heart can exhale, her voice can be heard, and her soul can heal. A godly husband is not just a provider of shelter but also a cultivator of safety. Emotional safety is not optional; it is sacred. It is the soil where intimacy grows, trust deepens, and love matures.

1. Emotional Safety: The Unseen Fortress

- **Safety is not silence; it is security.**
  A wife feels safe not when conflict is avoided, but when her emotions are welcomed without judgment.

- **Safety is not perfection—it's presence.**
  She doesn't need you to fix everything. She needs you to be with her in everything.

- **Safety is not control—it's compassion.**
  Emotional safety is built when a man listens more than he lectures, and comforts more than he critiques.

- **A safe home is a healing home.**
  When emotional safety is present, past wounds lose their power, and future dreams gain momentum.

2. Emotional Intelligence: The Husband's Hidden Strength

- Emotional intelligence is not weakness—it's wisdom.

Jesus wept. Jesus listened. Jesus lingered. Emotional maturity is Christlike maturity.

3. The Ministry of Presence: Healing Through Consistent Care

- **Presence is more potent than performance.**
  You don't need the perfect words—you need a faithful heart.

- **Consistency is the language of safety.**
  Show up daily, not just in crisis, but in quiet.

- **Touch her heart before you touch her body.**
  Emotional connection precedes physical intimacy. Pursue her soul.

- **Ask questions that open her spirit:**
  - "What's weighing on you today?"
  - "How can I support you this week?"
  - "What's something you wish I understood better?"

- **Be the man who stays.**
  Stay in the hard conversations. Stay in awkward silence. Stay when she's hurting. Stay when she's distant. Stay when she's vulnerable.

4. Healing Past Wounds: Love That Lingers

- **Your wife may carry wounds you didn't cause—but you can help heal them.**
  Trauma, betrayal, neglect, or abandonment may have shaped her story. Your consistent care can rewrite the narrative.

- **Healing takes time—and tenderness.**
  Don't rush her process. Be patient with her pain.

- **Apologize without defensiveness.**
  Own your mistakes. Repent with sincerity. Repair with action.

- **Speak life over her identity.**
  Remind her: "You are worthy. You are beautiful. You are safe with me."

- **Pray with her and for her.**
  Invite God into the healing. Let your home be a sanctuary of grace.

Closing Exhortation:

Brother, you are more than a husband; you are an anchor. In a world of emotional storms, your wife needs a harbor of safety. Be the man who listens deeply, loves gently, and remains faithful. Emotional safety is not soft—it is sacred. It is the ministry of Christ in your marriage. Let your presence be healing. Let your empathy be a strength. Let your love be her refuge.

Reflection

CHAPTER 4:
BUILDER OF TRUST

Trust is built brick by brick—through integrity, consistency, and humility. This chapter challenges husbands to be men of their word, transparent in their actions, and quick to own their mistakes. It also offers guidance for rebuilding trust after it's been broken.

CHAPTER 4

Builder of Trust

Integrity, Transparency, and Reliability as Spiritual Disciplines

Trust is not given—it's built. And when broken, it must be rebuilt brick by brick, moment by moment, day by day. A man of God is not measured by his charisma, but by his consistency. In marriage, ministry, and leadership, trust is the currency of influence. Without it, love erodes, respect fades, and intimacy dies. But with it, everything flourishes.

1. Trust Is Built, Not Assumed

- **Trust is earned through repetition, not reputation.**
  Your title doesn't guarantee trust—your track record does.

- **Trust is fragile but foundational.**
  It takes years to build, seconds to break, and a lifetime to repair.

- **Trust is the soil of intimacy.**
  Without it, your wife will guard her heart. With it, she will open her soul.

2. Integrity: The Unseen Strength

- **Integrity is who you are when no one's watching.**
  It's the alignment of your public life and private choices.

- **Integrity is not perfection—it's confession.**
  A man of integrity owns his failures, repents sincerely, and walks humbly.

- **Integrity is spiritual warfare.**

Every lie, every secret, every compromise is a crack in the foundation. Guard your heart.

"The righteous who walks in his integrity—blessed are his children after him." — Proverbs 20:7

3. Transparency: The Courage to Be Known

- **Transparency is not weakness, it's wisdom.**
  Secrets sabotage intimacy. Silence breeds suspicion. Honesty builds safety.

- **Be honest about your struggles.**
  Your wife doesn't need a perfect man—she needs a truthful one.

- **Invite accountability.**
  Trusted brothers, mentors, and spiritual guides help you stay clean, clear, and courageous.

- **Speak truth even when it costs you.**
  Truth may hurt in the moment, but deception destroys over time.

4. Reliability: The Ministry of Showing Up

- **Reliability is love in motion.**
  It's doing what you said you'd do, when you said you'd do it, how you said you'd do it.

- **Be predictable in your goodness.**
  Let your wife know she can count on you—not just in crisis, but in the mundane.

- **Follow-through is a spiritual discipline.**
  Jesus didn't just promise—He fulfilled. Be a man who finishes what he starts.

- **Small acts of reliability build massive trust:**

- Returning calls

- Keeping appointments

- Following up on emotional conversations

- Being present when you are tempted to withdraw.

5. Rebuilding Trust After Failure

- **Failure is not final, but it must be faced.**
  Denial delays healing. Defensiveness deepens wounds. Humility opens the door to restoration.

- **Rebuilding trust requires time, truth, and tenderness.**
  You cannot rush her healing. You must earn her trust again.

- **Apologize without excuses.**
  Own your actions. Validate her pain. Commit to change.

- **Let your actions speak louder than your apologies.**
  Words may start the process, but consistency completes it.

- **Invite God into the rebuilding.**
  Trust is sacred. Restoration is spiritual. Healing is holy.

6. Why Consistency Is More Powerful Than Charisma

- **Charisma may get you in the door—but consistency keeps you in the room.**
  Your wife does not need fireworks; she needs faithfulness.

- **Be the man who shows up, not just the man who shines.**
  Trust is built in the boring. In the daily. In the dependable.

Closing Exhortation:

Brother, you are a builder, not of walls but of trust. Lay each brick with integrity. Cement it with transparency. Strengthen it with reliability. And when you fail, rebuild with humility. Your consistency is your legacy. Your trustworthiness is your mission. Be the man on whom she can rely. Be the man God can trust. Be the builder who never stops building.

Reflection

CHAPTER 5:
SERVANT LEADER
IN THE HOME

Leadership in marriage isn't about control—it's about Christlike service. This chapter redefines headship through the lens of humility, sacrifice, and empowerment. Husbands learn to lead spiritually, emotionally, and practically by putting their wives' flourishing above their own comfort.

CHAPTER 5

Servant Leader in the Home

Leadership Modeled After Jesus: Sacrificial, Humble, and Empowering

Leadership in the home is not about dominance — it is about devotion. It is not about being served, but about serving. The godly husband leads like Jesus: with a towel in his hand, grace in his heart, and strength in his spirit. He does not demand respect — he earns it through humility, sacrifice, and love.

1. Jesus: The Blueprint for Leadership

"The Son of Man did not come to be served, but to serve..." — *Matthew 20:28*

- **Jesus led by laying down His life.**
  Authentic leadership begins with surrender, not control.

- **Jesus washed feet before He taught theology.**
  Servant leadership is not just spiritual—it's practical.

- **Jesus empowered others to flourish.**
  A servant leader lifts others higher, not himself.

- **Jesus balanced authority with tenderness.**
  He spoke truth with compassion, led firmly but gently, and never used power to intimidate.

2. Balancing Authority with Tenderness

- **Authority is not a license to dominate—it's a call to serve.**
  Headship in marriage is not superiority; it's responsibility.

- **Tenderness is not weakness—it's wisdom.**
  A tender man is emotionally safe, spiritually grounded, and relationally strong.

- **Lead with both backbone and heart.**
  Be firm in conviction, soft in tone, and steady in presence.

3. Practical Ways to Lead Spiritually, Emotionally, and Practically

Spiritual Leadership

- Initiate prayer with and for your wife.

- Read Scripture together and discuss its application.

- Set the spiritual tone of the home—worship, grace, and truth.

- Model repentance and spiritual hunger.

Emotional Leadership

- Be the first to apologize.

- Validate her feelings without rushing to fix them.

- Ask intentional questions: "How's your heart today?" "What's bringing you joy or stress?"

- Create space for her voice to matter.

Practical Leadership

- Share the load—clean, cook, organize, and serve.

- Manage time and resources with wisdom and generosity.

- Be proactive in solving problems, not passive or reactive.

- Lead in planning—date nights, family rhythms, and household decisions.

4. Building a Culture of Servant Leadership

- **Honor her publicly and privately.**
  Speak well of her in front of others. Affirm her in private.

- **Serve without scoreboard.**
  Don't keep track of who did what. Love keeps no record of wrongs—or chores.

- **Empower her gifts and calling.**
  Help her flourish in her passions, ministry, and purpose.

- **Be interruptible.**
  Jesus stopped for the hurting. Be willing to pause your agenda for her heart.

- **Lead with joy, not just duty.**
  Let your leadership be marked by delight, not drudgery.

Closing Exhortation:

Brother, you serve as the leader of your home, not because you're flawless, but because you are called to it. Lead with the humility, sacrifice, and strength demonstrated by Jesus. Be the man who prays before others, admits when he's wrong, and serves selflessly. Exercise gentle authority and empower leadership. Let your love be evident and loud. The world needs fewer rulers and more humble servants. Be the kind of leader who kneels.

Reflection

CHAPTER 6:
PROTECTOR OF PEACE

A godly husband guards the atmosphere of his home. This chapter explores how to shield your marriage from spiritual attack, emotional chaos, and worldly distractions. It includes practical strategies for cultivating rest, setting boundaries, and becoming a priest over your household.

CHAPTER 6

Protector of Peace

Guarding Your Marriage from Spiritual Attack, Emotional Chaos, and Worldly Distractions

Peace is not passive. No, it is fiercely protected and guarded. A godly husband is not just a provider or partner—he is a priest, a gatekeeper, and a guardian of the atmosphere of his home. He watches, prays, discerns, and defends. He does not just keep the wolves out—he cultivates rest within.

1. The Husband as Priest and Gatekeeper

"Watch over your heart with all diligence, for from it flow the springs of life." — *Proverbs 4:23*

- **Priest of the home:**
  Leads in worship, intercession, and spiritual discernment. He brings heaven's peace into earthly rhythms.

- **Gatekeeper of the home:**
  Guards what enters—media, attitudes, influences, and spiritual forces. He discerns what feeds peace and what fractures it.

- **Spiritual vigilance:**
  Recognizes that marriage is under constant spiritual pressure—temptation, distraction, division. He fights not with flesh, but with faith.

- **Emotional covering:**
  Creates safety by being emotionally present, responsive, and wise. He does not fuel chaos; he calms it and brings peace.

2. Guarding Against Spiritual Attack

- **Pray offensively, not just reactively.**
  Do not wait for a crisis—cover your marriage daily.

- **Discern spiritual patterns.**
  Is there a cycle of conflict before ministry moments? A heaviness during key decisions? If so, recognize and resist.

- **Use spiritual authority.**
  Declare peace. Rebuke confusion. Invite the Holy Spirit to reign.

3. Guarding Against Emotional Chaos

- **Be the emotional thermostat, not the thermometer.**
  Do not just reflect the mood—set it.

- **Listen deeply, respond gently.**
  Emotional safety is fostered through presence, not through performance.

- **Do not escalate—de-escalate.**
  When tension rises, lower your tone, slow your pace, and lead with grace.

- **Create rhythms of emotional connection.**
  Weekly check-ins, date nights, shared prayer, and intentional affection.

4. Guarding Against Worldly Distractions

- **Set boundaries around technology.**
  Phones off during meals. No screens in bed. Sabbath from media.

- **Protect sacred spaces.**
  The bedroom is for intimacy and rest—not conflict or clutter.

- **Simplify schedules.**
  Do not let busyness rob intimacy. Choose margin over madness.

- **Guard your gaze.**
  What you consume shapes your desires. Be vigilant with entertainment, social media, and visual purity.

5. Stewarding the Atmosphere of the Home

- **Speak life.**
  Your words shape the emotional climate. Bless, affirm, and encourage.

- **Create sacred rhythms.**
  Morning prayer, evening connection, weekly rest.

- **Be interruptible.**
  Peace is often found in the margins—be available for spontaneous connection.

- **Model repentance.**
  A peaceful home is not perfect. However, it is humble. Own your mistakes quickly.

Closing Exhortation:

Brother, you are the protector of peace. Not through force, but through faith. Not by control, but by covering. Your home is a sanctuary, and you are its priest. Guard it fiercely. Nurture it tenderly. Steward it wisely. Let your leadership embody spiritual alertness, emotional security, and sacred rest. Be the man who watches the gate, prays earnestly, and speaks peace over every room. The world may rage—but your home can be at peace.

Reflection

CHAPTER 7:
STUDENT OF HER SOUL

To love your wife well, you must know her deeply. This chapter invites husbands to become lifelong students of their wives—learning her story, understanding her fears, and celebrating her dreams. Curiosity becomes a form of intimacy, and compassion becomes a daily discipline.

CHAPTER 7

Student of Her Soul

Knowing Her Deeply—Her Story, Her Dreams, Her Fears

To love your wife well, you must learn about her—not as a project to fix, but as a mystery to cherish. She is not a puzzle to solve but a soul to understand. A godly husband becomes fluent in her emotional and spiritual language, listens with holy curiosity, and loves with deliberate compassion. Intimacy isn't built on proximity; it's built on pursuit.

1. The Sacred Call to Know Her

"Live with your wives in an understanding way…" — *1 Peter 3:7*

- **Understanding is not automatic—it's cultivated.**
  You do not drift into intimacy; you pursue it.

- **Knowing her is a lifelong journey.**
  Her soul is layered—story, wounds, dreams, desires, fears, and faith.

- **She is God's daughter before she is your wife.**
  Approach her heart with reverence, not entitlement.

- **You are not her savior, you are her student.**
  Learn her rhythms, her language, her longings.

2. Becoming Fluent in Her Emotional and Spiritual Language

- **Emotional fluency requires presence.**
  Don't just hear her words, feel her heart.

- **Spiritual fluency requires humility.**
  Don't preach, walk beside her.

- **Ask questions that open her soul.**
  "What's been heavy on your heart lately?" "What's something you're dreaming about?" "What's a fear you've been carrying?"

- **Listen without agenda.**
  Do not rush to fix, defend, or redirect. Let her be fully seen.

3. Curiosity and Compassion: The Twin Engines of Intimacy

- **Curiosity says, "I want to know you more."**
  It's the posture of pursuit, not assumption.

- **Compassion says, "I will hold what I discover with care."**
  It's the posture of safety, not judgment.

- **Ask, explore, and revisit.**
  Her story evolves—keep learning.

- **Don't just ask about her day—ask about her soul.**
  "What's something you're proud of this week?" "Where have you felt unseen?"

- **Celebrate her uniqueness.**
  Her quirks, passions, and preferences are not obstacles—they're treasures.

4. Practical Ways to Study Her Soul

Know Her Story

- Ask about her childhood, formative moments, and spiritual milestones.

- Understand her wounds—not to fix, but to honor.

- Learn what shaped her view of love, safety, and trust.

Know Her Dreams

- What does she long for spiritually, creatively, and relationally?

- What passions has she buried or postponed?

- How can you champion her calling?

Know Her Fears

- What triggers insecurity or anxiety?

- What lies does she battle internally?

- How can you speak truth and offer safety?

Know Her Faith

- What scriptures speak to her heart?

- What spiritual practices bring her peace?

- What doubts or questions is she wrestling with?

5. Building a Culture of Soulful Intimacy

- **Create space for soul talk.**
  Do not let coordination/planning dominate your marriage—make room for heart-level connection.

- **Be a safe place for her vulnerability.**
  Respond with grace, not critique.

- **Let her teach you.**
  Her perspective is a gift—receive it with humility.

Closing Exhortation:

Brother, your role is to study her soul deeply—not only her habits but also her heart, preferences, pain, strengths, and story. Approach her with sacred curiosity and love her with purposeful compassion. Strive to understand her emotional and spiritual language and communicate in it effortlessly. Aim for your marriage to be rich in depth, feeling secure, and filled with joy. Remember, she is not merely your wife but a lifelong lesson in love.

Reflection

CHAPTER 8:
STEWARD OF
SEXUAL INTEGRITY

Sexual integrity is foundational to spiritual authority. This chapter addresses purity, passion, and mutual respect in the marital bed. It offers healing for past brokenness, tools for guarding the heart, and a vision for honoring God through physical intimacy.

CHAPTER 8

Steward of Sexual Integrity

Honoring God with Your Body, Mind, and Desires

Sexual integrity goes beyond mere restraint; it embodies reverence. It is not just about avoiding sin but about practicing sacred stewardship. A godly husband honors God with his body, mind, and desires, fostering a culture rooted in purity, passion, and mutual respect. He heals from past wounds and commits to safeguarding his future faithfulness. More than resisting temptation, he redefines intimacy through the perspective of covenant love.

1. Sexual Integrity: A Sacred Stewardship

"You are not your own; you were bought at a price. Therefore, honor God with your bodies." — *1 Corinthians 6:19–20*

- **Your sexuality is not shameful—it's sacred.**
  God designed desire, but He also defines its boundaries.

- **Stewardship means ownership with accountability.**
  You are entrusted with your body, your thoughts, and your passions—not to indulge, but to honor.

- **Sexual integrity is holistic.**
  It includes your eyes, your imagination, your habits, your conversations, and your covenant.

- **Purity is not repression—it's alignment.**
  Aligning your desires with God's design leads to freedom, not fear.

2. Building a Culture of Purity, Passion, and Mutual Respect

- **Purity begins in private.**
  What you consume, imagine, and entertain shapes your desires.

- **Passion is not selfish; it is shared.**
  Pursue her heart, not just her body. Intimacy is emotional, spiritual, and physical.

- **Respect is the foundation of trust.**
  Consent, communication, and care are not optional—they're sacred.

- **Create a culture of safety.**
  Let your marriage be a place where both of you feel seen, heard, and honored.

3. Healing from Past Sexual Brokenness

- **God's grace is greater than your past.**
  No shame, no sin, no story is beyond redemption.

- **Confession is the doorway to healing.**
  Bring your story into the light—first to God, then to trusted community.

- **Healing is a journey, not a moment.**
  Be patient with the process. Consider counseling, accountability, and spiritual renewal.

- **Your past does not define your future.**
  In Christ, you are a new creation. Your story can become a testimony.

- **Invite your wife into the healing journey.**
  With wisdom and timing, share your heart. Let her be a partner in grace, not a stranger to your struggle.

4. Guarding Future Faithfulness

- **Set boundaries before temptation arrives.**
  Guard your phone, your media, your conversations, your travel.

- **Cultivate emotional intimacy.**
  Most sexual drift begins with emotional distance. Stay connected.

- **Be accountable.**
  Invite godly men to ask hard and challenging questions. Isolation breeds compromise.

- **Pursue your wife daily.**
  Do not let routine replace romance—practice of studying and learning more about her, loving her, delighting in her.

- **Pray for purity.**
  Ask God to renew your mind, cleanse your heart, and strengthen your resolve.

5. Practical Habits of Sexual Integrity

- **Do not just avoid sin—build virtue.**
  Fill your life with what is good and beautiful.

- **Let your marriage be a sanctuary.**
  A place of joy, safety, and sacred delight.

Closing Exhortation:

Brother, you are accountable for maintaining sexual integrity, not only for yourself but also for your marriage, legacy, and testimony. Respect God by caring for your body, thoughts, and desires. Cultivate an environment of purity, passion, and mutual respect. Heal from your past and protect what lies ahead. Make your intimacy sacred. Pursue it with joy. Let your story be one of redemption. The past is gone. You are free from desires. You are a child of the King. Steward this gift wisely.

Reflection

CHAPTER 9:
CULTIVATOR OF
JOY AND LAUGHTER

Joy is not optional—it's essential. This chapter celebrates the role of play, humor, and celebration in marriage. Husbands learn how to lighten the emotional load, create moments of delight, and rediscover the holy gift of laughter.

CHAPTER 9

Cultivator of Joy and Laughter

Why Joy Is a Spiritual Weapon and Laughter Is Holy

Joy is essential, not optional. Laughter has real value. A godly husband intentionally fosters joy and celebration, even in tough times and within marriage responsibilities. Joy matters—and you are meant to use it.

1. Joy: A Holy Resistance

"The joy of the Lord is your strength." — *Nehemiah 8:10*

- **Joy is not escapism—it's endurance.**
  It does not ignore pain—it defies despair.

- **Joy is spiritual warfare.**
  It silences cynicism, breaks heaviness, and invites heaven's atmosphere.

- **Laughter is holy.**
  It reflects the delight of God, the freedom of grace, and the intimacy of love.

- **A joyful home is a resilient home.**
  When joy is cultivated, conflict softens, connection deepens, and healing accelerates.

2. Levity Strengthens Love

Element	Impact of Marriage
Laughter	Builds emotional safety and connection
Playfulness	Sparks creativity and intimacy
Celebration	Honors milestones and cultivates gratitude
Humor	Diffuses tension and fosters resilience

- **Levity is not immaturity; it is intimacy.**
  When you laugh together, you bond deeper.

- **Shared joy builds trust.**
  Couples who laugh together recover faster from conflict.

- **Playfulness invites presence.**
  It pulls you out of routine and into relational renewal.

- **Celebration honors the journey.**
  It says, "We're still here. We're still us. And that's worth rejoicing."

3. Creating Space for Play, Celebration, and Delight

Play

- Be spontaneous—initiate games, adventures, or silly moments.

- Do not take yourself too seriously. Let her see your light-hearted side.

- Invite her into joy—dance in the kitchen, sing in the car, laugh at inside jokes.

Celebration

- Mark milestones—anniversaries, answered prayers, small victories.

- Create traditions—monthly date nights, seasonal rituals, surprise getaways.

- Speak gratitude. Celebrate who she is, not just what she does.

Delight

- Notice beauty—sunsets, music, shared meals.

- Invite joy into ordinary moments, coffee together, walks, and shared silence.

- Be present. Joy comes from attention, not distraction.

4. Building a Culture of Joy in the Home

- **Speak joy into the home.**
  Your words shape the emotional climate—choose delight over complaint.

- **Model joy in adversity.**
  Let your kids and wife see that joy is possible even in storms.

- **Protect joy from erosion.**
  Guard against cynicism, busyness, and emotional drift.

Closing Exhortation:

Brother, you bring joy and laughter into life, not because life is simple, but because love makes it worth celebrating. Fill your home with happiness, not just responsibilities. Allow your marriage to be filled with laughter, not only routines. Joy sustains you, and laughter leaves a legacy. Be the man who dances freely, celebrates fully, laughs loudly, and loves deeply. In a world often heavy, be a bright spark of joy.

Reflection

CHAPTER 10:
MENTOR TO THE
NEXT GENERATION

Your marriage is a legacy in motion. This chapter challenges husbands to model godly manhood for their children and spiritual sons. It explores fatherhood, generational blessing, and the power of living a life that preaches louder than words.

CHAPTER 10

Mentor to the Next Generation

Modeling Godly Manhood for Sons, Daughters, and Spiritual Sons

You are not only living for today but also shaping the future. Every word you speak, every decision you make, and every act of demonstrating godly manhood plants a seed for the next generation. Whether you are raising sons, daughters, or spiritual sons, your life functions as a blueprint. Your marriage communicates a message. Your legacy starts today.

1. Modeling Godly Manhood: More Caught Than Taught

"Follow me, as I follow Christ." — *1 Corinthians 11:1*

- **Children do not just hear your words—they absorb your ways.**
  Your tone, your habits, and your priorities—they become their framework for manhood, womanhood, and worship.

- **Model strength with tenderness.**
  Show that masculinity includes humility, emotional safety, and spiritual depth.

- **Model repentance and grace.**
  Let them see you apologize, forgive, and grow. Perfection doesn't build trust—authenticity does.

- **Model servant leadership.**
  Let them see you serve your wife, your church, and your community with joy and consistency.

2. Fathering with Intentionality and Legacy in Mind

- **Fatherhood is not just provision—it's formation.**
  You're shaping character, faith, and future.

- **Be present, not just available.**
  Presence means attention, engagement, and emotional availability.

- **Speak life into their identity.**
  Tell your sons who they are in Christ. Tell your daughters what godly love looks like.

- **Create legacy moments.**
  Retreats, rites of passage, letters, blessings—mark their journey with intentionality.

3. Your Marriage Preaches Louder Than Your Sermons

- **Your marriage is a living sermon.**
  It teaches your children what love looks like, what safety feels like, and what covenant means.

- **Conflict resolution models emotional maturity.**
  How you handle disagreement teaches them how to handle life.

- **Affection and honor model relational health.**
  Let them see you delight in your wife, speak well of her, and serve her joyfully.

- **Consistency builds credibility.**
  If your public ministry outshines your private marriage, your message loses weight.

- **Hospitality and joy create a culture of grace.**
  Let your home be a place where laughter, prayer, and peace dwell.

4. Building a Legacy That Lasts

- **Legacy is not what you leave behind—it's who you raise up.**
  Your children and spiritual sons will carry your values, your faith, and your example.

- **Mentor intentionally.**
  Invite younger men into your life. Share your story. Walk with them through theirs.

- **Live with the end in mind.**
  What do you want your children to say about your love, your leadership, your legacy?

Closing Exhortation:

Brother, you serve as a mentor to the next generation. Through fatherhood or spiritual leadership, your life serves as a message. Demonstrate godly manhood by leading with intention. Let your marriage speak louder than your words. You are constructing more than just a home—you are cultivating a legacy. Be the man they remember with gratitude, follow with confidence, and honor with joy.

Reflection

CHAPTER 11:
WARRIOR IN PRAYER

A godly husband fights for his family on his knees. This chapter equips men to become intercessors—praying for their wives, children, and homes with authority and consistency. It includes prayer strategies, spiritual warfare insights, and encouragement for building a prayer altar in the home.

CHAPTER 11

Warrior in Prayer

Interceding for Your Wife, Your Marriage, and Your Household

Before you defend your family on Earth, first defend them in prayer. The strongest tool a husband possesses isn't his voice during arguments or his physical strength during challenges—it's his kneeling prayer. You're not only a protector physically but also a spiritual warrior. Your prayers influence the atmosphere, dismantle strongholds, and invite divine blessings into your home.

1. Interceding for Your Wife: Cover Her in Prayer

"Husbands, love your wives, just as Christ loved the church and gave himself up for her to make her holy…" — *Ephesians 5:25–26*

- **Pray for her heart.**
  That she would feel safe, seen, and deeply loved.

- **Pray for her mind.**
  That anxiety, fear, and lies would be replaced with peace and truth.

- **Pray for her calling.**
  That she would walk boldly in the gifts and purpose God has placed within her.

- **Pray for her protection.**
  That the shield of your intercession would repel every spiritual attack.

- **Pray with her, not just for her.**
  Let her hear your voice calling heaven down on her behalf.

2. Interceding for Your Marriage: Guard the Covenant

- **Marriage is a spiritual battleground.**
  The enemy hates a covenant. He will attack unity, intimacy, and trust.

- **Pray for oneness.**
  That your hearts would be knit together in grace and truth.

- **Pray against division.**
  Rebuke the spirit of offense, bitterness, and isolation.

- **Pray for joy and laughter.**
  That your home would be filled with the fruit of the Spirit.

- **Pray for generational impact.**
  That your marriage would model Christ's love and leave a legacy of faith.

3. Building a Prayer Altar in Your Home

"Then the Lord said… 'Build an altar to the Lord your God…'" — *Judges 6:25*

- **Your home is not neutral ground—it's holy ground.**
  Build an altar where heaven meets earth.

- **Teach your children to pray.**
  Let them see you cry out to God, not just talk about Him.

- **Make prayer a culture, not a crisis response.**
  Normalize spiritual warfare, thanksgiving, and prophetic declaration.

4. Spiritual Warfare Begins with a Kneeling Husband

- **You are the gatekeeper.**

What you allow in your home spiritually begins with your posture.

- **Kneeling is not weakness—it's warfare.**
  Every time you bow, you rise in authority.

- **Your prayers dismantle darkness.**
  Rebuke the enemy. Declare truth. Release peace.

- **Your humility invites heaven.**
  God resists the proud but gives grace to the humble.

- **Your intercession is priestly.**
  You stand between your family and the forces that seek to destroy them.

Closing Exhortation:

Brother, you are a warrior in prayer. Your authority isn't in your title—it's in your surrender. Build a prayer altar—intercede with fire. Kneel with power. Let your home be a fortress of faith, your marriage a testimony of grace, and your legacy a lineage of intercessors. The battle is real—but victory belongs to those who kneel.

Reflection

CHAPTER 12:
FINISHER WITH HONOR

The goal isn't just to start strong—it's to finish well. This final chapter calls husbands to live with eternity in view, leaving behind a legacy of faithfulness, love, and godliness. It ends with a pastoral charge to rise, remain, and reflect Christ until the very end.

CHAPTER 12

Finisher with Honor

Faithful to the End. Legacy in Love. Eternity in View.

You were never meant to begin with boldness only to fade away. Your call is to finish with integrity. The test of a godly man isn't in initial passion but in sustained faithfulness. Your concluding chapters are significant. Every choice, sacrifice, and act of love shapes your legacy. Strive to finish strong—not just for your reputation but for His honor.

1. Finishing Well: Faithful to the End

"I have fought the good fight, I have finished the race, I have kept the faith." — *2 Timothy 4:7*

- **Faithfulness is the crown of manhood.**
  Not perfection, not popularity—faithfulness.

- **Finish your race with integrity.**
  Stay true to your vows, your calling, your convictions.

- **Don't coast—contend.**
  The final stretch is often the hardest. Press in. Stay alert. Stay humble.

- **Guard your heart from drift.**
  The enemy doesn't need you to fall—he wants you to fade.

- **Let your final years be your finest years.**
  Pour wisdom into others. Mentor. Bless. Speak life.

2. Leaving a Legacy of Love, Leadership, and Godliness

- **Your legacy is not what you leave behind—it's who you leave behind.**
  Sons, daughters, spiritual sons—what will they carry from your life?

- **Love that outlasts your lifetime.**
  Let your wife and children remember your tenderness, your prayers, your pursuit of their hearts.

- **Leadership that multiplies.**
  Equip others to lead. Pass the baton. Raise up men who will run farther than you did.

- **Godliness that echoes.**
  Let your life be a sermon that continues to preach long after you're gone.

3. A Final Charge: Live with Eternity in View

"Only one life, 'twill soon be past; only what's done for Christ will last."
— *C. T. Studd*

- **Eternity recalibrates everything.**
  Your time, your money, your marriage, your ministry—it all matters in light of forever.

- **Live for the well-done.**
  Not applause, not comfort, not success—but the voice of the Father saying, "Well done, good and faithful servant."

- **Invest in souls, not just stuff.**
  Your legacy is measured in transformed lives, not accumulated possessions.

- **Let heaven shape your home.**
  Pray like eternity matters. Love like time is short. Lead like souls are at stake.

71

- **Die empty.**

  Pour out every gift, every word, every act of love. Leave nothing buried.

4. A Husband's Benediction

"Blessed is the man who trusts in the Lord, whose confidence is in Him." — *Jeremiah 17:7*

Let this be your final charge:

- Love your wife with unwavering devotion.

- Lead your children with holy intentionality.

- Serve your church with quiet strength.

- Mentor younger men with open hands.

- Finish your race with fire in your bones and grace on your lips.

Let your life be a lighthouse. Let your legacy be a map. Let your final breath be a declaration: *I have finished with honor.*

Reflection

Conclusion

Legacy in Every Cell

A godly husband embodies more than just a role; it's a calling, a covenant, and a space where heaven meets earth. His character isn't shaped by perfection but by continuous striving: a grace-filled pursuit to mirror Christ in every thought, decision, and sacrifice. Rather than conforming to cultural standards, he responds to the cross's call—to die daily, love sincerely, and lead with humility.

This book has explored themes of spiritual integrity, emotional maturity, servant leadership, and covenantal love. However, the measure of this DNA lies beyond theory — it resides in legacy. It is evident in how his children pray, how his wife thrives, and how his home transforms into a sanctuary rather than merely a shelter. Ultimately, it's reflected in how his influence on life persists long after his departure.

To every man reading this: you aren't merely building a marriage, but a monument to grace. Your love for your wife goes beyond just affection; it reflects the heart of God. Raising children isn't only about nurturing; it's about sending arrows into a broken world.

Allow your DNA to express itself more powerfully than words. Ensure your love endures beyond your lifetime. Let your legacy be inscribed not only in history but also in eternity.

www.ingramcontent.com/pod-product-compliance
Lightning Source LLC
Chambersburg PA
CBHW032359280326
41935CB00008B/634